HELI-SKI THE CARIBOOS AND MONASHEES –
A Photographic Odyssey and Practical Guide

By Neal and Linda Rogers

HELI·SKI

THE CARIBOOS AND MONASHEES

A Photographic
Odyssey
and
Practical Guide
to
Helicopter Skiing
in
British Columbia

By Neal Rogers
   Linda Rogers

Special Thanks to
   Mike Wiegele
   Mark Thompson
   Leonard Eckel
   Ken Lieberman
   Mary Comba
   Hans Gmoser
   Madeline Daniel
   Erich Schadinger
   Tad Derbyshire

First published in 1986 by

Earth and Great Weather Publishing Co.
202 South Montana Street
Butte, Montana 59701

Graphics and production by Len Visual Design, Helena, MT

Library of Congress Catalog Card Number 85-90535
ISBN: O-934318-78-6, cloth, O-934318-79-4 softcover
Distributed by Falcon Press, P.O. Box 279, Billings, MT 59103
Second printing
Printed by Dai Nippon, San Francisco
Printed in Japan

BLUE GLASS GLACIER–MONASHEES.

To the guides
and pilots who have
taken us safely through
the mountains

Preface

Back in 1965 Hans Gmoser of Canadian Mountain Holidays pioneered skiing by helicopter in the Bugaboo Range of British Columbia. Since that time multiple areas have been developed in the British Columbia Rockies from Panorama in the south to Valemont in the north. The deepest snow areas are in the Cariboo and Monashee ranges, which are the first to catch the moisture after it passes the coastal ranges of the Pacific. Each company has hundreds of square miles in its ski area. This privilege is granted to them by the Canadian government. As with other skiers, my first exposure to stories of this skiing was associated with the Bugaboo Lodge. Since this was the first of all the areas, it has the most notoriety. Almost every skier in the world knows something about heli-skiing near the Bugaboo Spires.

Mention the Cariboos and Monashees and most people nod approvingly, but they really don't know how special this region is. I've been fortunate enough to make runs in these mountain ranges. **It is true** that there is deeper snow here, deeper than any other region in the Rockies. The tree skiing is beyond belief with steep runs down which you can glide easily or jump effortlessly when conditions are right (most of the time). When the weather is clear the glacial scenery is unbelievable. Skiers in the know come from Canada, the USA, Europe, and Japan to ski the special runs like Steinbock, Big Red, Most Magnificent, and Steep Mother.

Each trip is a new encounter–fascinating people, diverse weather patterns, and new mountains to explore. I've personally skied at Mica Creek, the Cariboo Lodge, and with Mike Wiegele. Most of my experiences in recent years have been with Mike Wiegele and his crew at Blue River, British Columbia. My friend-ship with Mike has grown over the years, and he has taught me a great deal about the high mountains in the winter. I have spoken to guests and compiled statistics and stories over the years. I'd like to say that each trip was perfect, but it was not. The weather determines that. I plan to go skiing in the mountains whatever the conditions. I just hope that my week is the great one that I dream about, and 80% of the time it is.

Helicopter skiing takes place at 1800 feet (550 m) and above in the British Columbia Rockies. The altitudes below 3500 feet (1065 m) are prone to warm temperatures except in January and February most years.

It seems that in early season, January-mid-February, most skiing is done in the trees with occasional trips to the high glaciers. As March approaches, the snow depth increases, wind decreases, and it is sunnier. The high glaciers are most accessible and are skied more often. Tree skiing fades as the warmer temperatures crust up the snow at lower altitudes. Each skier has his special preference, but the weather really determines the character of the trip. Good powder can be found into May in good years.

If you fly and ski every day, everyone is happy. If the weather is bad, groups tend to get a little morose at times. In the past years, some of the areas began using Bell 214 helicopters, which eliminate many of the problems of flying in difficult weather. These have tremendous horsepower and can whisk 11 skiers and a guide straight up a mountain side to the drop off point. Lesser-powered machines had to circle in wide arcs to gain altitude, limiting their ability to fly in marginal weather. New pickups at 3500 feet (1065 m) have been cut in all the ranges, and down days happen less often.

For the past 15 years, my friends have known how compulsive I am about watching the weather. They know I've been monitoring Willard Scott daily to predict the conditions we would have when the time came to ski in January. From September to January friends are always asking me if it's raining in Blue River. They know they'll get a short summary of the conditions in B.C. at that very moment. They enjoy teasing me because they all remember too well the year we drove into Blue River in a raging rainstorm.

Blue River is a small logging town nestled between the Cariboos and Monashees. It is similar to other heli-ski towns in B.C. that quicken a powder skier's pulse–Mica, Revelstoke, Valemount, Nakusp. This region of the Rockies gathers more snow in one winter than most other ski areas get in 2-3 seasons. Mike Wiegele started his company in Blue River upon confirmation of an old Indian legend telling of "big snow flakes falling straight down." It was, indeed, a windless, snow-filled corner of the Rockies.

The only problem was that on my arrival in Blue River it was raining cats and dogs. With all my planning and predictions I couldn't believe the weather would do this to me. Only 20 minutes outside of town it had been snowing heavily. The snow banks there were 10-15 feet high. Snow on the tops of railroad cars idle for the winter was as high as the cars themselves. Powder snow was dumping out of a low dark cloud ceiling. I couldn't believe the weather could change so rapidly, but it did. The weather has a way of doing what it wants. I was depressed.

Luckily, what I forgot to throw into all my permutations, combinations, and predictions was that at higher altitudes with colder temperatures it was snowing heavily. The glaciers and upper tree runs were being blanketed with the powdery stuff you dream about. That week turned out to be the finest ski week I've ever spent in the mountains. Fortunately, low avalanche danger prevailed.

One day on a mountain top in the Cariboos I jumped out of the helicopter into fluffy snow as deep as my armpits. All day we skied the steep and deep glacial runs with snow tapping on goggles, demanding windshield wipers. We jumped off cliffs into 20-foot depths of feathery fluff. We laughed and skied some more. All this and two days before it was "raining in Blue River."

As you can see, the weather will determine what type of trip you're going to have. CMH and Mike Wiegele have superb operations with everything taken care of except the weather.

I look at each trip as a true adventure and learning process. You start each week with education about mountains and avalanches. **Safe, controlled** skiing is emphasized. Learning about different types of snow conditions and how to ski the trees without much effort take a few trips to learn. Training each other with avalanche rescue radios and learning avalanche strategies takes four hours at least. Almost every operator in Canada has had a fatal accident at some time over the years. My personal feeling is that you must realize there is a risk any time you fly in helicopters and ski in an uncontrolled environment. All my guides have been experienced, and I know that all possible precautions have been taken. Avalanche technology is still in its infancy, and, despite the best intentions, avalanches and accidents do happen. Thankfully, they are quite rare.

I really appreciate all the efforts that the owners, guides, and employees of the companies have put in over the years for people like me and other skiers who want to taste the finest powder skiing in the world.

Introduction

by Mike Wiegele

I was very excited when Neal and Linda asked me to write an introduction to their book. I've been looking at Neal's slides for eight years now and have been impressed by the beauty captured in them each successive year. Now Neal and Linda have combined the images into a story and are giving others an exquisite invitation to this mountain realm they have discovered.

In my brief lifetime I've witnessed a total revolution in mountaineering. Wilderness back-country skiing has become accessible by the helicopter – a wonderful machine contrived by man's magnificent intelligence. Almost by the whim of one's thought, you are airlifted to the powdery slopes one used to only dream about. We can now visit almost any place and not alter anything except the silence. Gone are the images of the old-time explorer. The helicopter has removed the agony of carrying heavy bags over treacherous steep places and exposing oneself to constant danger. To many, the drudgery of putting one foot in front of the other, time after time, became a type of pleasure. How else was there a way to get to the tops of high peaks? Dreams of our wildest fantasies 30 years ago have come true. Mountains that took weeks to approach and days to climb are scaled in mere minutes. What had taken a whole winter's exploration on foot can be accomplished in one beautiful day flying in the helicopter. The ecstasy of this experience cannot be matched. Flying and skiing in the beautiful Rockies of British Columbia is a wonderful gift that God has given us. In appreciation we name these exquisite places Paradise and Most Magnificent.

Another revolution has taken place in the traditional method of guiding in the mountains. The guide's approach is now done on a scientific basis rather than by intuition and feel as had been the practice of the past. The risk of mountaineering is still there – as it always was and ever will be. But now we can go only for the rewards. Alertness, quickness, and precision are more demanded to deal with the risks inherent in the back-country. Computers are now used to store records and analyze our observations from the field. We concentrate on the evaluation of hazards, especially the avalanches. We're getting to know the snow – how it behaves, how it stabilizes or develops weak layers. All of this brings us a little closer to nature and makes us feel a bit more comfortable in the mountains.

The essence of guiding is to be in harmony with the environment. Every visit we make to the mountains is a privilege and a gift. Sometimes the natural environment of the backcountry can be quite hostile and frightening. Most skiers coming here have grown up in an urban setting and are virtually unattuned to the secretive and delicate warnings of the mountains. It is the guide's job to help them to blend in and become a secure integral element of the wilderness. We never want to challenge the mountains or their various moods.

To me the improvements in ski equipment have now made the downhill portion as enjoyable as the exploration and flying. The multitude of surface conditions gives us some of the greatest challenges in skiing. Luckily we encounter powder snow 85% of the time.

People are fascinating to watch. At ski areas they can make 10-15 turns in powder snow and be ecstatic. With the helicopter we can provide runs of 300 turns, day after day, for a whole week. We can approach 5-10 different mountains a day or, on the great days, 15 or more. That is more than a climber can do in an entire year. Yet sometimes their faces tell me that they are not satisfied with their accomplishments. One of my greatest thrills is to watch these people undergo a transformation and begin to comprehend what a special gift nature has given them. They begin to understand that backcountry skiing is not always perfect and start to see beauty in the changing moods of the mountains. They notice the differences in light, the movements of the shadows, and the thrill of just being there. Their faces light up as though they had just received their first puppy. When I can share one of my special places with them, I am overjoyed. We just ski – nobody has to say anything – a mutual bond of mountaineers has formed between us.

I think Neal and Linda will impart those same feelings to you as you read the pages of this book. I hope I can share them with you in person in seasons to come.

Mike Wiegele
January 1986

MIKE LOOKING FOR HIS NEXT RUN
IN POWDER PARADISE.

Go for it!

You may be one of those people who finds getting up in the morning an excruciating experience—not so on this particular morning. When the alarm goes off you hit the floor with a feeling of anticipation and exhilaration. Outside your window the snow lies invitingly white and soft. It's quickly into some clothes and off to breakfast, the snow crunching cheerfully beneath your shoes as you make your way to the dining room. All around you are sun, blue sky, sparkling snow, and magnificent peaks to dazzle the eye and kindle the imagination.

Opening the door to the dining room reconnects you with the real world—the smell of coffee and bacon, the buzz of excited voices, and the clink of silverware. Breakfast must vie for space in your stomach with all those butterflies.

An expectant hush falls over the room as Mike, the boss of this outfit, steps in. He welcomes you with his characteristic cheerfulness and understatement. "The snow looks pretty good today. We've had two meters new over the past few days and the weather forecast shows clear weather at least for today. We'll plan to meet at 8 o'clock for the Pieps drill. Be ready to ski after that."

It's difficult to concentrate on a teaching session when your heart is already making turns in the deep powder, but there is no other more important hour to be spent in preparation for heli-skiing. During the hour you will learn how to handle yourself and your equipment around the helicopter. They are wondrous machines, and it is because of their capabilities that this kind of skiing in the back country exists, but they can also be dangerous to those who are careless.

You will also learn about avalanche danger, minimizing that hazard, and what to do in the event of a slide. You were issued a Pieps transmitting device at the welcome session the night before.

MARTIN HEUBERGER DISCUSSING RESCUE STRATEGY IN CASE OF AN AVALANCHE.

Your guide's voice brings you back to the task at hand–locate your skis, clean off boot soles and step into the bindings–not easily done in thigh-deep powder. Somehow it doesn't even occur to you to complain about this kind of work. Last pre-flight checklist before blast off–Pieps in place and transmitting, boots buckled, bindings latched, gloves OK, goggles OK. Your guide outlines the plan of attack for the slope below, and then he drops away in graceful, slow-motion turns. He stops below and calls for you to come down. You feel compelled to plunge right in, afraid that somehow all of this could disappear if you don't hurry. The first turn a little rough; the second; the third, and then the rhythm is there. Sinking into the crystalline white, billowing over your shoulders and into your face, then rising up into sunshine and blue sky and laughter, you feel you could go forever and the elation is almost too much to contain. When you reach your guide you wish there were words to tell him about this magical thing you have experienced, but the look on your face and the faces of the others in your group says it all.

All those months of planning and preparation were worth it, as this experience exceeds your highest expectations.

Too good to be true? Don't you believe it. Nearly every skier we've spoken with has this special feeling about their heli-skiing experience.

Our desire to share this unique experience with you, the reader, stimulated the production of this book. We agree with the old saying that a picture is worth a thousand words. This book is a month-by-month odyssey through the winter of helicopter skiing. At the end of the book you will find factual information on the subject which we hope you will find helpful in planning your own heli-skiing adventure.

Now you will learn how to be sure that it is sending a signal at all times while you are skiing. Your guide will discuss the method of conducting a search in the event of an avalanche and how to use your Pieps as a homing device to locate a buried skier as quickly as possible. It's a sobering thought to realize that your life depends on the other people in the group and their lives depend on you. That thought gets tucked away in the back of your mind to keep silent vigil as you ski.

And then it's time to fly. The helicopter surges to life, its intimidating rotor blast reminding you of the power of the beast. Into the cabin, door latched, seatbelts on, and then you lift off. As the motel, parking lot, and then the town drop away below you, a surge of adrenalin boosts your pulse and makes your palms wet. You look across the cabin at the other tense faces and realize that you're all feeling that mixture of fear, excitement and anticipation.

Ahead you see mile upon mile of valleys, forests, glaciers, and mountain peaks extending to the horizon. The sound of the rotor blades changes and you realize that your pilot is settling the machine into a berth on a ridge top. Out of the helicopter, crouch in the snow with your group, and then feel the blast of wind as the rotor blades slice the air to lift away.

The first thing you become aware of after the helicopter leaves is–silence. Your group almost seems to be momentarily held in suspended animation in the nearly palpable quiet. Then–laughter, crunching snow– the spell is broken, and you stand to take your first look at this vast, frozen paradise. Peaks stretch away in all directions as far as the eye can see. Intense white and blue hurts your eyes. Below your feet, snowfields roll and tumble to the forests far below.

Cariboo and Monashee Country

THIS PAINTING BY MURRAY HAY REPRESENTS A SMALL PORTION OF THE CARIBOO AND MONASHEE
RANGES. THE ORANGE LINES REPRESENT POTENTIAL SKI RUNS. THERE ARE THOUSANDS OF OTHER
MOUNTAINS AND RUNS THAT ARE NOT SHOWN.

Dominion Creek

Moonbeam Creek

Serpentine Creek

Howard Cr.

n Creek

Foster Cr.

e Creek

Creek

Mud Creek

Adams River

January

WEATHER/SNOW AND AVALANCHE CONDITIONS

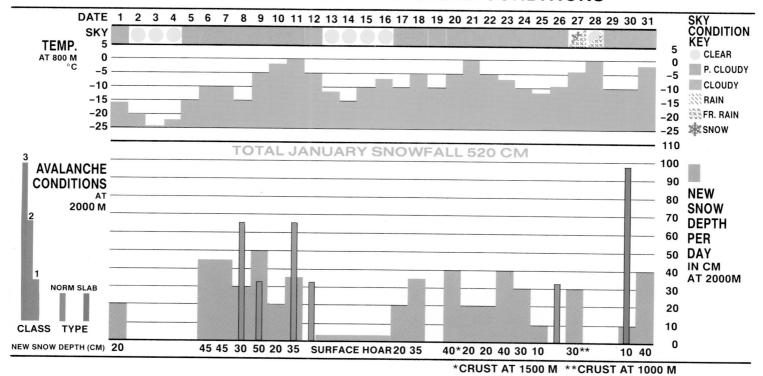

DATE 1 2 3 4 5 6 7 8 9 10 11 12 13 14 15 16 17 18 19 20 21 22 23 24 25 26 27 28 29 30 31

SKY

TEMP. AT 800 M °C

5 0 -5 -10 -15 -20 -25

SKY CONDITION KEY
- CLEAR
- P. CLOUDY
- CLOUDY
- RAIN
- FR. RAIN
- SNOW

TOTAL JANUARY SNOWFALL 520 CM

AVALANCHE CONDITIONS AT 2000 M

3 2 1

NORM SLAB

CLASS TYPE

NEW SNOW DEPTH PER DAY IN CM AT 2000M

NEW SNOW DEPTH (CM) 20   45 45 30 50 20 35   SURFACE HOAR 20 35   40*20 20 40 30 10   30**   10 40

*CRUST AT 1500 M   **CRUST AT 1000 M

SUN DOGS AND SNOW GHOSTS—MICA CREEK, MONASHEES

-25° Sundogs

My early January trip to CMH's Mica Creek was highlighted by a 10-foot base at the Mica Hotel. I knew immediately that I was with the right bunch of skiers the moment I found out that my German roommate, Thomas, had climbed the north face of the Eiger.

Temperatures hovered at -15° to -25°C all week. It isn't supposed to snow heavily at those temperatures, but it did! Each night outside our window we placed a meter-long, stretched-out, wire hanger. Every morning snow climbed half way up it or more–light, fluffy-puff snow.

Warm helicopter interiors were really appreciated that week. Twelve people suffered some mild form of frostbite. The worst case was two blackened toes on a vascular surgeon who felt compelled to smoke cigarettes in those temperatures.

STEEP AND DEEP–MICA CREEK.

This all sounds foreboding, but the skiing was superb. The weather put on an outstanding light show. Snow crystallized out of blue sky, forming multi-colored sundogs. The air was as clear as I've ever seen it; cross-lit trees and mountains were a photographer's dream. Skiing was dynamite, with 3-4 feet of new snow daily in the trees. Whooshing through the forests of Big Red and Steep and Deep are memories I'll never forget.

SUNDOGS AT -25°C.

One year at Mica it snowed 12 feet in town during the week I was there. Skiing was chest or neck deep most of the time. Because of the huge snow falls, we couldn't ski every day. On one of my exploratory jaunts I met a snowplow operator who told me that one season they had 69 feet (21 meters) of snow in town. Mica is 1800 feet (550 meters) above sea level. If you multiply 69 feet x 3 to get the snow depth at 6000 feet (1827 m) above sea level, you get 207 feet (63 m) or 2484 inches (6300 cm). Divide that by the 120 days of winter = 20 inches (51 cm) of new snow a day every day in the mountains. WOW!

OUTSIDE THE OLD MICA HOTEL, 1 METER OF NEW SNOW OVERNIGHT.

COLD EVENING SNOW STORM APPROACHING – MONASHEES.

January is not always -25 °C. Some years it has rained up to 3000 meters above sea level.

ELEVATOR RUN AT MICA.

Smokin' in the trees!

Very cold days
are still loaded with fun

CONCORDE – FIRST TURN OF THE MORNING AT -30°C.

This was my "cold trip" to Mica Creek. I treasure it because of the intense beauty of the frigid Monashees in January.

-30°C IN THE MONASHEES.

At very cold temperatures the warm helicopter is a welcome sight after each run.

LATE AFTERNOON

Pow Pow!

NEAL ROGERS IN THE MONASHEES.

Flying in the January cold is an exhilarating experience. The atmospheric light shows fade as warm February approaches.

February

WEATHER/SNOW AND AVALANCHE CONDITIONS

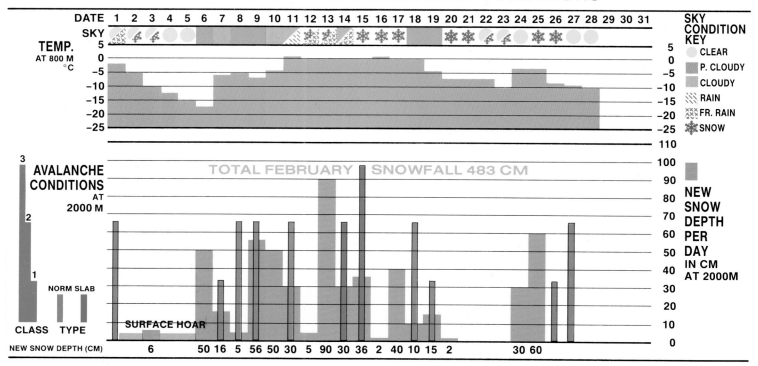

DATE	1 2 3 4 5 6 7 8 9 10 11 12 13 14 15 16 17 18 19 20 21 22 23 24 25 26 27 28 29 30 31

TEMP. AT 800 M °C

SKY CONDITION KEY
- CLEAR
- P. CLOUDY
- CLOUDY
- RAIN
- FR. RAIN
- SNOW

AVALANCHE CONDITIONS AT 2000 M

TOTAL FEBRUARY SNOWFALL 483 CM

NEW SNOW DEPTH PER DAY IN CM AT 2000M

CLASS — TYPE (NORM SLAB)

SURFACE HOAR

NEW SNOW DEPTH (CM): 6   50 16 5 56 50 30 5 90 30 36 2 40 10 15 2   30 60

MIKE WIEGELE STARTING A DAY IN THE CARIBOOS.

24

BRUNO SCHADINGER—NORTH BLUE RIVER RUN—CARIBOOS.

February can
bring anything
from wild days
in the trees to

TENY DEANE ON DAMN DEEP—CARIBOOS.

JACK ATCHESON ON CEDAR RUN—MONASHEES.

. . . high glacial paradise

ON TOP OF THE WORLD – PARADISE IN THE MONASHEES.

PARADISE GLACIER, MONASHEES.

My first day of heli-skiing was in February

LINDA ROGERS ON NORBERT'S NOSE – CARIBOOS.

"Is that your Pieps beeping away like crazy, or your heart rate?"

That's my guide speaking. What am I doing here? I'm so nervous I can hardly walk, let alone ski. I feel like I'm in an astronaut suit instead of a ski suit. Ever have one of those dreams where you're trying to get somewhere and you feel like your legs are bogged down in mud? That's me, except I'm wide awake, standing on the top of a mountain somewhere in British Columbia and looking for the easiest way down.

Funny how you can psyche yourself up for something prior to the event, only to suffer terrible pangs of anguish when the time arrives. I was like that. I travel with a crowd of pretty hot skiers. That's not to say that I'm a hot skier–I just travel with them.

When they all signed up to go heli-skiing, I just sort of kept traveling along and signed up, too. Once that deed was done, it didn't seem like all that awesome a task. After all, surely not every skier who goes on one of these adventures can be a clone of Jean-Claude Killy.

I spent the entire summer, fall, and early winter convincing myself that I was definitely heli-ski material. I'd followed my freinds down most of the hairy ski slopes of the western ski resorts, and I just knew I could cut it.

Then came the moment of truth in the Cariboos. I had purposely asked for a group to ski with who wouldn't be out to set new records for most vertical feet, biggest jumps, and greatest overall craziness, but I still felt pretty overwhelmed that first morning.

You discover in a big hurry, however, that there are no multiple choice answers to your dilemma. There's only one way down . . . to ski. That puts things back in perspective.

I certainly would not have won many style points that first run–you don't look real terrific trying to ski deep powder in a snowplow. I did make it down, however, and as I looked back up the slope we had just completed I realized that maybe this wasn't "Mission Impossible" after all.

By the end of the week I had indeed found my niche. My group didn't ski the most vertical feet, and we certainly didn't always look like material for a Warren Miller ski movie, but we had a wonderful time, formed good friendships, and discovered that, after all, we were pretty good skiers. As testimony to what a wonderful time I had, I've been back every year.

"SKI WELT" IN THE MONASHEES.

PAYING HOMAGE TO "THE MACHINE."

Cloudy, snowy days are February's call to ski the trees

Cloudy, snowy days in the past meant you didn't ski. But with a Bell 214 helicopter and better landings and pickups you now have access to the trees. These are the days when THE MACHINE puts you down at the top of a windless forest. Jump out . . . and you immediately sink down to your waist. You know what's coming up and it is fantastic! Skiing in the trees allows you visibility in fog and low light. The snow blows over your head with every turn. You can see only part of the time—goggles rattle as endless waves of snow patter them with each push of the skis. You breathe only once in a while because snow fills your nose and mouth . . . sometimes leaving you wishing there was a snorkel in your mouth instead of in your suitcase.

Numerous times you become magically airborne with only a soft landing to stop you. Through the fog you hear your guide's whistle and steer your way toward him. Ghosts of skiers pop out from behind trees to regroup. You laugh together for a moment then jump back into the ecstasy of falling with only your body and skis to hold you back from truly flying.

ALMOST NECK DEEP—GARY KELTZ IN REDMONDS FOREST.

TRIS STONGER "TWISTIN'" ON DUFFY'S—MONASHEES.

CEDAR RUN, MONASHEES.

A SKI GHOST.

Cloudy days get frisky; feather soft
landings bring out crazy moves

ERICH SCHADINGER
"JUST SHOWIN' OFF"
MONASHEES

As early February progresses winds may keep the high glaciers unskiable. This is when the wind-protected tree runs are at their best.

J.V. PRUNSKIS ON STEINBOCK.

✗ CEDAR RUN IN THE MONASHEES.

✗ "CRUISIN' " NORBERT'S NOSE – MONASHEES.

Tree skiing

You wish that you could be an animal of infinite grace and strength as you glide silently through the trees. It is an encounter with elemental sensations. You hear the snow hissing quietly over the tips of your skis; the call of your partner through the trees; and the distant chirp of your guide's whistle indicating the way down. You feel the cool air rushing against your face and see the alternating flashes of sunlight and shade as you move down through the forest. You can even smell the crisp, clean fragrance of the pines as you go by.

The tree runs in the Canadian Rockies are generally fairly open stands of pines and some cedars. The slopes vary in steepness but almost all include natural jumps formed from large stumps and boulders. These make a great playground when covered with up to twenty feet of snow. It is a simple matter to spring gently off of one of these launching pads knowing that you will land with a soft "pooff" at the bottom, your landing cushioned by all that snow.

These runs are one of the special calling cards of the Cana-dian Rockies. There is no other place that I know of that can reproduce that kind of terrain and consistently cover it with piles of fluffy snow.

As with any other part of the helicopter skiing experience, there are things to get used to, precautions to take, and inherent dangers in the terrain, but what a thrill to be in such a place! Because the trees separate you to some extent from the sight and sound of the members of your group, it becomes a very personal experience between you and the mountain.

MIKE WIEGELE–STEINBOCK.

Steinbock are a unique goat who have a habit of jumping amazing distances up and down mountain sides. The ski run named for this particular goat is a series of natural jumps from 5 to 30 feet high. Jumping from lump to bump to lump goes on for endless vertical feet when the conditions are right. There's another run called Cathedral with so much air that there aren't any flat spots. Some year when the conditons are right I'll get my chance to ski it.

I will always remember my first run on Steinbock, which, incidentally, was the first run I ever skied at Blue River. The snow was thigh deep and soft. Mike Wiegele, who was my guide that day, turned his head, winked, and said, "Follow me!" We started onto an open slope with lots of small bumps. Yelling and screaming, I went wild. Suddenly, the bottom dropped out–I was 15 feet in the air and could only see a small ledge which Mike had just glided over. I touched on the ledge but couldn't stop there. Another 15 feet later I landed. Somehow I kept my balance and skied over to Mike who was by now laughing wildly. "Great run, eh?" Wow! It couldn't have been better.

Forest Cruising

Tree skiing is sliding through the forest of evergreen and cedar. Sometimes the pitch is a gentle 20-30° and one can just glide along with no effort at all. It's best when the powder is a little firm. On numerous occasions I've run into little air pockets of cedar scent while passing through these grey-barked mammoths hung with moss. The quiet and serenity relaxes you so much that you forget that you're traveling on a pair of skis.

Magical evening light on
Cedar Run in the Monashees

Part of the magic of tree skiing is the really big bumps!

Some skiers will do anything for a picture. This is especially true of my friend Bruno Schadinger whose brother Erich is a great guide and famous photographer. This particular day on Steinbock, Bruno came to a 40-foot ledge which just dropped away. Right off the top was a series of staircase bumps leading to a ledge halfway down. From there it was airtime. Erich and I had taken another line and had come out by the landing site. Erich tried to guide Bruno down this skiable line, but Bruno didn't get the message. His first turn was 20 feet down on the ledge, and from there it was a "garage sale." I'll never forget Bruno's first words after an 8-point landing. "#*¢& you, Erich!"

It's hard to believe that a man with two children would ski like this, but then, most of you have never skied Steinbock–yet.

1 →

3

4

5

2

Lower Most Magnificent is next to Steinbock . . .

Lower Most Magnificent is next door to Steinbock. The upper part is 3000 vertical feet on the glacier. This lower part is 2500 feet in the trees. I tricked my friend Gary Keltz into jumping off this one. Normally you can see over the edge of most of the jumps. This one was quite high and the bottom couldn't be seen. I had just skied under the lip and knew the landing was almost perfect—tons of soft snow, but flat. Gary was a little hesitant. I knew it would make a great picture and encouraged Gary to go for Big Airtime. He did—all 25 feet of it.

LOWER MOST MAGNIFICENT.

40

O..O...O...O...H H H BABY!

Skiing the trees or the glaciers is strenuous work

Getting wet is a big part of "Chopper" skiing. You'd think that this comes from falling into the neck-deep stuff, but it isn't always. Tight collars, snow cuffs, and long-armed gloves help solve that problem.

The major source of wetness is sweat–plain old hard work sweat. Working hard at skiing produces gallons of the stuff. Temperatures in the B.C. Rockies hover most of the time above 15°F. Cold butts are common along with soaked backs.

I don't understand, however, why the guides are always dry. They must wipe roll-on deodorant over their entire bodies before they go out in the morning–or perhaps they don't work at it as hard as the rest of us mortals.

Gortex type materials allow a good portion of this sweat to evaporate into the air. I'm convinced that this moisture then condenses into clouds which make powder snow. It's great to know that I'm contributing to the snow pack while I'm skiing.

It takes special pilots to fly groups of skiers in the trees and the high mountains

GREG CURTIS FLYING "THE MACHINE."

I've flown with many pilots over the past ten years, each one very skillful and very experienced. Each one was also a character and a half—a true "piece of work." Most have had three to four thousand hours of experience, a lot of that in the mountains. Learning the subtleties of the wind, updrafts, downdrafts, air pockets, and thermals takes a lot of time. The touch needed to fly THE MACHINE is a very delicate one. Add to all of that the changeable weather in the mountains and you can see that you have one very smart cookie flying you around.

HIGH FLYING IN THE CARIBOOS.

Runs get higher and longer as the late February winds die down

TOO MANY TO COUNT!—UPPER MOST MAGNIFICENT, CARIBOOS.

CEDAR RUN—MONASHEES.

MOST MAGNIFICENT, CARIBOOS.

"SKI WELT," MONASHEES.

Each frame of film
freezes a special moment
forever

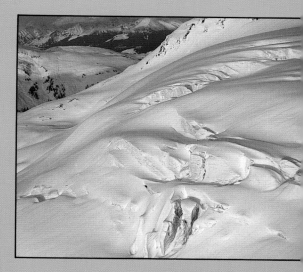

Some moments are special . . . like "Big Tuesday" February 27

This was the best day in our entire ski career. Deep windless fluff in the Cariboos and dazzling sunlight.

THUNDER RIVER RUN – CARIBOOS.

Why are these people smiling? They just finished 22,000 vertical feet of skiing on Big Tuesday and it isn't even lunchtime yet.

ARE WE HAVING FUN YET?

49

SPECTACULAR SCENERY NEAR THE CARIBOO LODGE.

Longer days lead to even bigger things in March

FIRST TRACKS EVER ON PARADISE GLACIER AT MICA CREEK IN THE MONASHEES.

March

WEATHER/SNOW AND AVALANCHE CONDITIONS

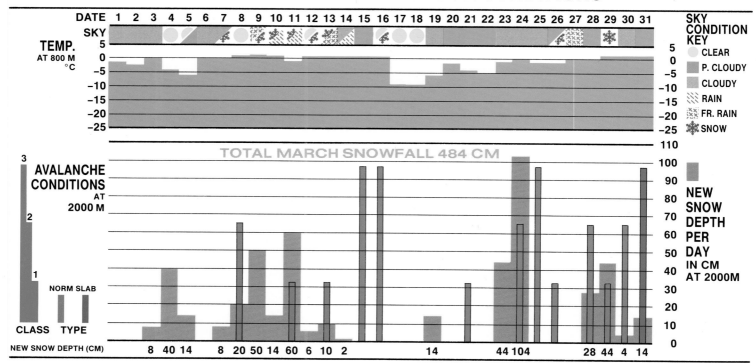

TOTAL MARCH SNOWFALL 484 CM

NEW SNOW DEPTH (CM): 8 40 14   8 20 50 14 60 6 10 2   14   44 104   28 44 4 14

BRIAN NATTRASS ON MT. ALBREDA RUN—MONASHEES.

MORNING LIGHT ON THE GLACIERS ABOVE THE CARIBOO LODGE.

In early March, cool clear nights form hoar frost

The combination of clear, calm, cold nights in March makes surface hoar build up on top of the snow. These six-sided flakes can grow to ½ inch in diameter.

The early morning sunshine sparkles its way through the prismatic crystals. Skiing it feels like magically sliding over the smoothest velvet in the world.

JANE BATTENBERG – MOST MAGNIFICENT – CARIBOOS.

ERICH SCHADINGER – CARIBOOS.

54

Warm March afternoons bring conditions that can be less than perfect. Here a windy, wet storm dropped 3 inches of ice crust to 9000 feet (2750 m) above sea level.

MY FAVORITE SKI SURFACE, "DEATH CRUST."

Long March days allow groups to really get to know each other

It seems that every trip's adventure coalesces people into encounter groups with bizarre names. Team Machine, The Awesome Bavarian Skiing Machine, Team Shred and the Hackers are a few that I've come in contact with. You depend on, interact and play with a diverse group of international people over the course of a week. The first few days everyone wants to be the best skier, get the deepest snow and have the most turns. After three days you realize that there is plenty of everything to go around. The groups then form a close knit bond among themselves. The guides recognize this phenomenon and try to place people of compatible skiing ability and personalities together as early as they can in the week. This is a tough job especially when snow conditions aren't perfect.

Whenever I leave for home, I always have a big lump in my throat and a feeling of sadness. My group has accomplished more than a skiing adventure. It's always hard saying goodbye to close friends.

A lady's point of view

"Where's the bathroom?" A reasonable question.

"Are you crazy, lady? We're miles from the nearest town. There aren't any rest areas handy, either. Up here you'll have to find a rock or lean up against the nearest tree."

One of the distinguishing characteristics of the feminine gender is our notable lack of bladder capacity. Couple that with the structure of our anatomy which makes it nearly impossible to manage a bathroom stop in a typical ski suit. That's not to mention the added challenge of making that bathroom stop leaning against a pine tree or huddling down behind a boulder.

Men have absolutely no sympathy for you in that situation, either. They should have to try it our way sometime.

One particular glacier run has earned the name Nancy's Relief. It is extremely long, about 3000 vertical feet and extremely open. The immortal Nancy skied all day with a bursting bladder trying to avoid the embarassment of having 10 men in her group watch her relieve herself. By the time this run was over, she couldn't take it any more and dove behind the first available snow bank.

Have you ever tried skiing for a whole day with a full bladder? Don't. I'm an expert on all the ways to try to avoid needing a potty break while out skiing–not drinking any fluids, going to the bathroom every five minutes before you leave in the morning, skiing very smoothly and trying not to fall–none of them work.

All these concerns and a few others go through your mind when you're approaching your first experience as a feminine addition to a heli-skiing trip.

Here are the facts.

There absolutely are not any bathrooms available in the heli territory. If you're lucky, an obliging helicopter pilot will let you use his machine for cover to take a pit stop during lunch. I've learned that it pays to keep one eye over your shoulder, however. I've had an occasional pilot get a big charge out of turning on the prop and thereby filling my ski suit, which at that point was gathered around my ankles, with snow. Snow feels just terrific on a bare bottom.

Unless you bring your own team of lady skiers, you're certain to be heavily outnumbered by men in any of the heli-ski bases. It can be a bit intimidating at first, but, just think, where else can you have that kind of attention? It gets even better when they discover that you can really ski after all.

The owners and managers of the operations like the idea of having women participating in this sport. They have been unfailingly supportive, helpful, and kind to me. That doesn't mean that you won't be in for some good-natured ribbing. The men get that as well.

My single most important piece of advice for the lady heli-skier, aside from being sure you have tissue in your pocket for that emergency bathroom stop, is to approach the entire venture with a firm grip on your sense of humor and the intention to have a good time. I guarantee you will have fun.

Clear skies allow
the helicopter
to fly far into the
backcountry

THUNDER RIVER–CARIBOOS.

MOONRISE
IN THE MONASHEES.

58

March is really the month to explore the glaciers

RON WERNER–PARADISE GLACIER–MONASHEES.

SKI WELT – MONASHEES.

MOON RUN – CARIBOOS.

"TEAM SHRED" – MONASHEES.

Is for fun with friends

DENNIS AND JEFF WAGNER, FATHER AND SON – MT. ALBREDA – MONASHEES.

PARADISE GLACIER – MONASHEES.

There is a special thrill in being able to stand on the top of a mountain and look out across the rest of the earth around you. The only others who get to experience this are mountain climbers and eagles. Skiers have the luxury of being delivered to this magical place on the rotor blades of a helicopter. It seems a bit like cheating, but you'll never hear me complain.

Skiing the glaciers is what heli-skiing is all about. It is a totally unique environment, coupling wide open snowfields covered with powder, surrounded by magnificent mountains and icefalls. Here you find the steep, deep, and untracked powder for which the Canadian Rockies are famous. You and ten friends can frolic in the fluff and fulfill your wildest dreams about skiing.

"WILLI" ON DOMINION CREEK – MONASHEES.

CADILLAC'S DESCENT – CARIBOOS.

Flying through glacier country
is as beautiful and exciting as
the skiing.

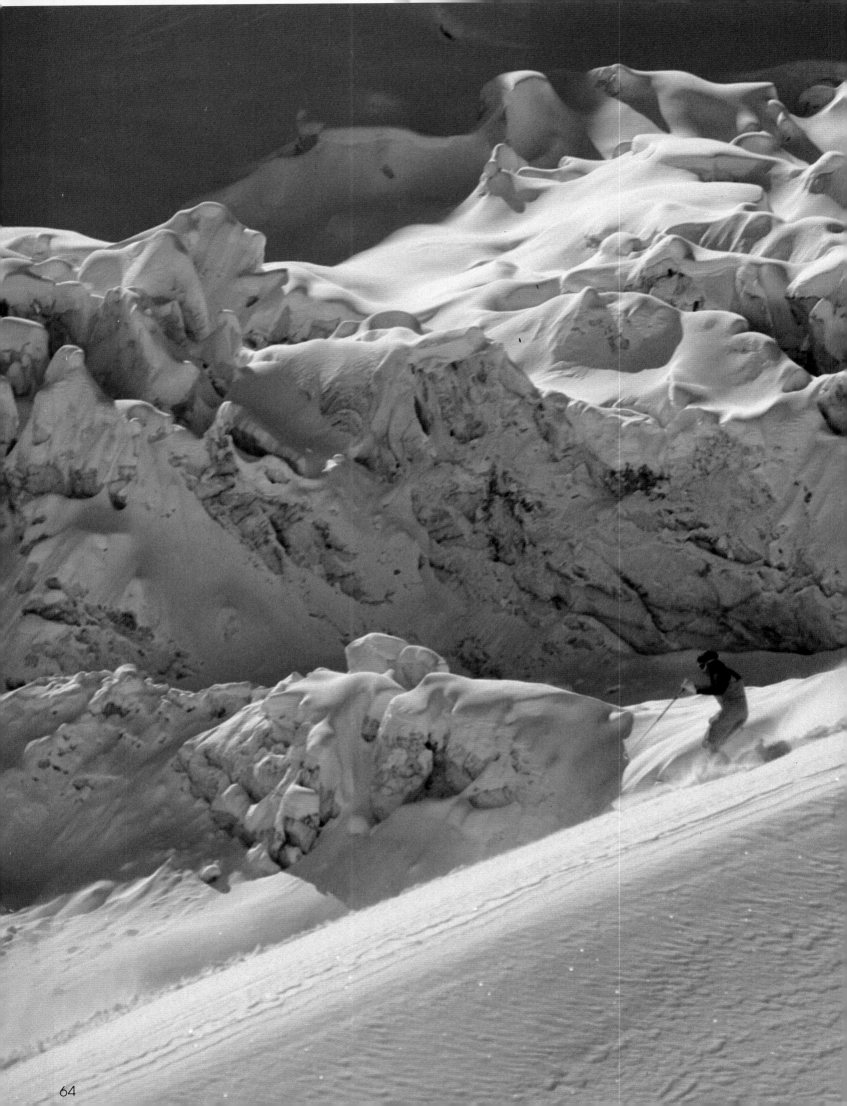

Icefalls on Paradise Glacier

The scale of the place is over-whelming. It is difficult to absorb just how massive the mountains and glaciers are. These stark blue massifs excite my soul with a time-less intensity found nowhere else on earth.

Skiing steep rolls on the glaciers is exhilarating. They can be so steep that every turn causes snow to surface release. You have to ski just fast enough to keep the sliding snow from tripping you up.

On the flats all you need is a pair of cruising skis and a lot of speed

Getting to the run is half the fun

JUMP FOR JOY!

CEDAR RUN–MONASHEES.

Every moment when the sun shines is a visual delight!

Some years the snow in open, tree-lined valleys is superb even very late in March.

MARTIN HEUBERGER—CARIBOOS.

BOB HEATH—BIG WHITE—CARIBOOS.

The magical helicopter can fly you from sunrise to sunset through the most beautiful terrain in the world.

FIRST LANDING OF THE DAY ON CEDAR RUN. ✕

SUNSET IN THE MONASHEES.

Starting off on
a 5,000-foot
descent—
Paradise Run—
Monashees

Making Tracks

Mount Albreda is a prominent peak on the road from Valemont to Blue River. It is one of the most photogenic places I know. When the weather is right, 4500 feet of vertical can be attained. The so-called "Team Machine" made these S tracks in perfect conditions. It takes an abnormally compulsive bunch of skiers to ski this tightly. On my drive home I could see these tracks five miles away outlined on Albreda's flanks. I stared at them for 20 minutes trying to etch them permanently into my brain, knowing that a coming storm would soon erase them forever.

MOUNT ALBREDA – 3535 M (11,600 FT) X

Glacial sunsets in late March
sometimes leave me speechless

"I HOPE MY PARACHUTE OPENS!" BRIAN NATTRASS—MONASHEES.

April

WEATHER/SNOW AND AVALANCHE CONDITIONS

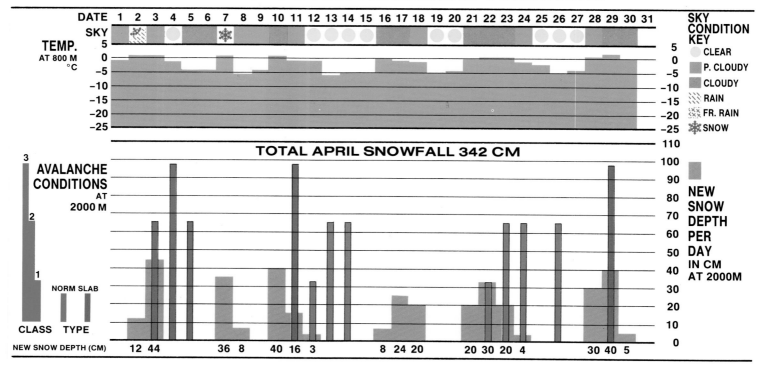

| DATE | 1 | 2 | 3 | 4 | 5 | 6 | 7 | 8 | 9 | 10 | 11 | 12 | 13 | 14 | 15 | 16 | 17 | 18 | 19 | 20 | 21 | 22 | 23 | 24 | 25 | 26 | 27 | 28 | 29 | 30 | 31 |

TEMP. AT 800 M °C

SKY CONDITION KEY
- CLEAR
- P. CLOUDY
- CLOUDY
- RAIN
- FR. RAIN
- SNOW

TOTAL APRIL SNOWFALL 342 CM

AVALANCHE CONDITIONS AT 2000 M

CLASS   TYPE
NORM SLAB

NEW SNOW DEPTH PER DAY IN CM AT 2000M

NEW SNOW DEPTH (CM)   12 44   36 8   40 16 3   8 24 20   20 30 20 4   30 40 5

SCOTT ROWED – MOST MAGNIFICENT – CARIBOOS.

A DEEP DAY ON CADILLAC'S DESCENT—CARIBOOS.

April can have exceptional variations in weather. Soft powder in the trees or on the glaciers can happen anytime.

Warmer weather sometimes brings rain into the valleys.

BIG WHITE—CARIBOOS.

ALOHA BOWL – MONASHEES.

■ A skier can ski corn snow in the morning

■ Get a tan at lunch

■ Ski Champagne Powder in the afternoon

■ And also catch a last run on a northwest facing powder slope in the Alpenglow!

JOHN ARNOW – PARADISE RUN
OFF TO AN EVENING RUN – NANCY'S RELIEF – CARIBOOS.

When the weather is stable and clear, the high glacial runs are exceptional

NOTE THE TRACKS ON THE MIDDLE SLOPE—AN UNNAMED RUN IN THE MONASHEES.

FIGURE 8s—CARIBOOS.

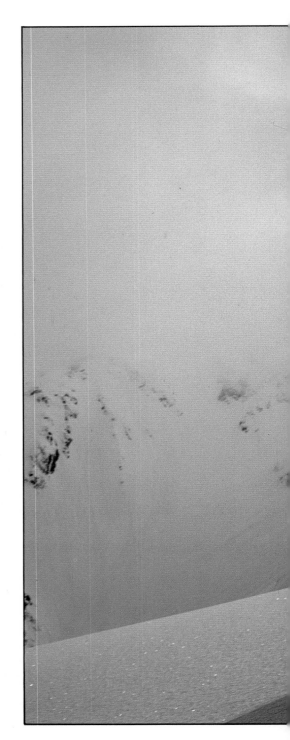

The crystal sharp images will always be etched in my brain

BOB HEATH ON BIG WHITE – CARIBOOS.

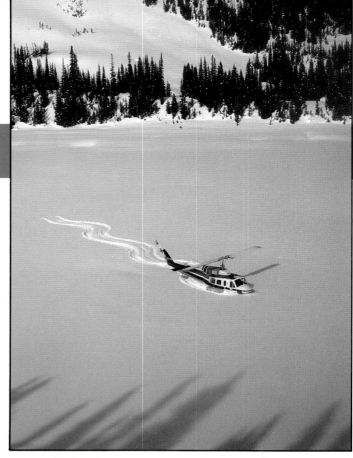

The nice weather lets the pilots "loosen up." On some days they turn as well as the skiers.

TUAN HO PUTTING IN "S" TRACKS IN THE MONASHEES.

ONLY 4000 VERTS TO GO—MONASHEES.

Springtime is fun time— April anecdotes abound!

"Hey, Bruno! Bruno, come here, please!" These words ordered my buddy and hot skier Bruno Gubetta to join his friendly guide Erich Schadinger at the head of the pack. We were skiing a 4000 vertical foot run in the Monashees through a beautiful series of ice falls. When Bruno arrived he was politely ordered to hand over one of his skis to a fellow in another group who took a tumble and lost one of his skis over a 2000-foot cliff. Without a word Bruno kicked off his ski and took off. If you look closely, you'll notice Bruno skiing on one ski. He skied the remaining 2000 vertical feet knee deep, without missing a turn. Awesome!

BRUNO ON GALAXY—MONASHEES.

Clear April
weather lets a
pilot take you
where no man
has been before

GREG CURTIS
DEFYING GRAVITY OVER MUD GLACIER
– MONASHEES.

he April sun would last forever

ERICH SCHADINGER AND LINDA ROGERS ON MUD GLACIER–MONASHEES.

CEDAR RUN – MONASHEES.

The long sunsets
of April set the
stage for very
special
moments

As always the sun drops
toward the horizon, bringing the
greatest memories I have of skiing
... the runs in the deepening
alpenglow of evening.

As you can tell, I love skiing late in the day. As the sun's angle gets lower, the light casts first a deep yellow, and then a deepening orange glow onto the mountains. The snow gleams pink and the air stills. Shadows get longer and the contrasts of light, ski suits and sky become highlighted. The best pictures always seem to happen at this time because of the rich colors. I hurry from blue shadows to sunlit openings to capture the skiers as they glide by. Since we've been out all day the guides know the snow conditions very well. They always save a run with super snow for the last run down to "Miller Time." On very special days the helicopter flies you to a series of runs into the sunset, each snowfield a little further west, with deepening alpenglow on each successive run. This goes on until the sun slips below the distant mountains and all turns to shadow. Somehow evening seems quieter and more personal. As the fading light plays its spectrum of colors across the snow, I'm making my last few turns of the day. I can feel the almost pleasant ache of fatigued muscle combined with a sense of accomplishment and quiet pleasure. I look forward to dry clothes, cold beer, and hot food—and another day tomorrow.

Twilight time in the Monashees

Now that April is over, let's prepare for next season

EQUIPMENT

This appendix is meant as a guide to clothing and equipment. It is in no way complete and is not foolproof. It should give you a good idea how to heli-ski in relative comfort through weather conditions that are infinitely variable. The main concept is safety, comfort, and fun.

SKIS

The best powder ski ever made for heli-skiing is the so-called "Fischer Fat," otherwise known as Rounders, Futuras, or Futura Extremes. They are not performance skis. They are designed for fun. I've seen them take a fair to average powder skier and transform him into a comfortable expert in a morning. They don't do well in breakable crust or hard pack, but are passable in those conditions. Women usually use 160-180 cm. lengths; men 180-190 cm.

The best all around ski for a variety of snow conditions—powder, crust, wind slab, etc.—is the Blizzard Powder Guides Edition in the 190-205 cm lengths. These are a bit more demanding than the Fischers.

Better skiers gravitate toward longer performance-type skis. These work well, but demand more work on the part of the skier. Anyone not in top shape will fatigue in 2-3 days and need to move to the shorter, more forgiving skiis. The longer, stiffer skis don't float on the surface well and take more leg effort to function efficiently. When you assume you may ski 25,000-30,000 vertical feet a day in deep snow, you have to be prepared.

3-PINNER PENELOPE STREET IN THE MONASHEES.

Most heli-ski areas have skis for rent. If you don't own or want to buy a pair of powder skis, use the rentals.

Only strong 3-pin skiers should apply. Bring the best possible equipment and all replacement parts.

BINDINGS

Buy the best binding you can get. There is no binding specifically indicated for heli-skiing. Ski on your bindings before your heli-trip to be sure they are functioning properly.

EXTRA HINTS

A good wax job saves effort climbing and walking, as does good bottom maintenance.

Check bindings yourself before skiing. Be sure you can twist out of them—test this with your ski boots on and the help of a friend.

Silicone spray helps keep snow from sticking to bindings and boots.

BOOTS

Comfortable, broken-in boots are the only way to go. This is not the time to begin wearing a new pair. On cold days (0° to -25°F) boot muffs may help. They apply a layer of insulation to the outside of the boot. A good pair of ski boot orthotics is the best investment you can make. A custom fit insole provides instant contact with the ski. The best part is that you don't have to severely tighten the boot to get this contact, thus optimizing good circulation and warm toes.

POLES

Most areas provide special avalanche poles that screw together and function as a probe in case of avalanche. **Don't use straps** when skiing in the trees. Poles hook on branches and dislocate shoulders.

CLOTHING

The best principle is to dress in layers. Temperatures can be -25°F to +50°F, so come prepared. Usually the temperature is about +15°F in the morning and about +30°F in the afternoon. On an average day, you might wear long underwear, a warm high-neck turtleneck, and a one-piece lightly insulated suit.

Underwear–Polypropylene or Capilene is best as it wicks perspiration away from the skin. For temperatures above 15°F wear a thin pair; for temperatures below 15°F a heavy pair. Wool is acceptable, but cotton and other fabrics keep you wet, and therefore, you may get colder as the day progresses.

Suits–Wetness comes from two places–sweat and snow. A suit that breathes is best. Fabrics like Gortex and the like work well, but need to be cleaned to work efficiently. One-piece suits are best on cold, deep-powder days. They work best for keeping the snow out. Good boot and glove cuffs are important. A high collar helps to keep the snow out of your neck. On cold days, below 10°F, a down vest would be helpful for added warmth.

On spring days a two-piece suit is a good idea so that you can shed the jacket.

Wipe as much snow off your outfit as you can before getting into the helicopter. The temperature inside is 40-50 °F and the snow melts–it can soak you to the bone.

Socks–Polypropylene socks keep your feet dry and warm. Two

Usually by mid-day most gloves and mittens are wet despite sealants, etc. An extra pair carried in a fanny pack is well worth the effort. You will find that you will need to dry your gloves or mittens in your room each night in preparation for the next day. Gloves and mittens insulated with some of the synthetic fibers are a bit easier to dry than wool, down, and leather.

and the use of fog cloths. This can be very frustrating in a setting where visibility is a joy as well as a necessity.

Contact lenses are infinitely better than eyeglasses in all situations. You will encounter the same difficulty in fogging your glasses as you will your goggles.

FANNY PACK

A small pack is quite useful–it should be carried with you at all

LET'S GO SKIING!–CARIBOOS.

light pairs work well on cold days. Wool and silk socks also work well. Here again, try to experiment before your trip to find the combination that works best for you to provide warmth and comfort.

Gloves–Any good warm gloves work well. Mittens are especially good for cold days. Gloves and mittens with long cuffs to keep the snow out of your wrists are better because they stay dry longer.

Glove liners are a good idea for added warmth on days with temperatures below 0 °F.

GOGGLES

The better designs are those that are sealed with foam to keep the snow out. The best goggle is the Bollé, period! It just won't fog if properly taken care of. Never use a fog cloth on them.

The turbo types with fans are a second choice. The rest all fog despite manufacturer's claims

times. You can carry extra gloves, handkerchief, lip balm, binding key, matches, extra clothing for cold days, camera, film, lens cleaner for goggles, fog cloth, knife, and any other items you might need during the day. Remember, the helicopter does not make runs back to base camp because you forgot something.

You've got to be prepared for anything from tired muscles to the infinite variations of the weather

Cycling is a good method to improve leg strength, especially if you can do so on hilly terrain so that you are doing a great deal of uphill pedalling.

Many skiers get "powder wrist"–a tendonitis resulting from the jarring pole plants. Good arm strength helps prevent this injury, as does time spent skiing deep snow to get used to the difference in the pole plant. Treatment is wrapping the wrist, aspirin, and, if it is severe, rest.

3. Skiing–Ski hard for at least one week before your trip at a

CONDITIONING

This is the most important aspect of preparing for your trip. The biggest disappointment is to be sore and stiff after one day of skiing and face the rest of the week in pain. Plan to ski hard for seven days, all day. You will ski more safely when you are in good condition as well as being able to continue learning without getting fatigued.

1. Aerobics–Aerobic exercise conditions the heart and lungs and helps significantly with endurance. Work up to 35-40 minute workouts daily before your trip. This will not, however, develop the leg and arm strength needed.

2. Leg and arm strength–Use Nautilus or other weight training programs to develop this strength. Start slowly and work up to a comfortable level. If you don't desire to weight train, do a quarter squat (half to full squats are hard on the knees) and begin hopping side to side with the feet together, hopping higher and wider to make the exercise more difficult. Start with 50-100 of these two times a day and work up to 500 three times a day. One fifty-year-old lady skier told me she did 5000 of these a day to get in shape.

Work out your arms, also. The poling is more strenuous than you might think.

challenging area near your home. You'll gain confidence, strength, and agility and know whether your equipment is working properly.

4. Expertise–Most heli-ski operations cater to the non-expert skier in several ways. You will generally be placed with a group of other skiers of similar ability. This allows you to ski a bit more slowly and get used to the conditions. Your guide will give progressive instructions as the week goes along if you let him know you are there to learn. You can learn more powder technique in one week of heli-skiing than at a ski area in two months.

Your whole trip is determined by the weather

Over the years I have encountered all extremes of weather in the Cariboos and Monashees. I've seen rain to 9000 feet (2750 m) in January

10-year Statistics

Good Snow (6" of powder) happens 50% of the time.

Excellent Snow (12" of powder) happens 20% of the time.

Outstanding Stuff (2-3 feet or more of snow) occurs 10% of the time.

Poor Skiing Crust, Slab or even no skiing occurs 20% of the time.

Plan to have 1-2 days down due to poor weather conditions.

These percentages were gathered over a long period, not one week's experience. We fly more now with the 214 helicopters, which can fly in marginal weather conditions.

Old snow, especially on north slopes, stays in good shape for weeks because of altitude and dry air. Three-week-old snow is like cruising on a velvet sheet. The skis slide and turn with no effort at all.

Altitude plays a huge role in what type of snow you ski. Sometimes the upper two-thirds of a run is perfect, 2-3 feet of soft fluff, but as one goes lower a hard crust and ice layer forms and skiing then becomes a formidable adventure.

As you can see, a week can provide huge variations. My attitude now is "Expect the worst"—80% of the time you'll be wrong!

APPROACHING STORM—MONASHEES.

and March, and encountered -30° C temperatures for a whole week. It snowed 12 feet in one week at 1500 feet above sea level and we couldn't ski. It snowed 8 feet another week and we skied every day in perfect powder. Snow quality ranges from 2" of ice crust, to wind slab, to the finest champagne powder one can imagine. Last year we skied corn snow on the glaciers in 70° temperatures in April.

The most dangerous aspect of the weather is how it causes avalanches

The thought of avalanches is always on my mind. The more I'm out in the back country, the more respect I have for the mountains. One gets the impression from the media that all avalanches are always big. A small, 40-foot slide could bury a skier forever. I am amazed how much work goes into snow safety. The guides' lives revolve around avoiding avalanches the whole winter.

I've been lucky. I've never been in a slide. Last season I skied during the highest hazard the guides had seen for many years. Every precaution known to man was taken. Yet we had fun, safe skiing during these high-hazard conditions. I have the utmost respect for all the guides that I have skied with. After all, they have spent a large portion of their lives in the mountains protecting themselves and their clients from nature's wrath.

I'd like to give you a brief description of the precautions that are taken to protect the skiers.

One must realize that the British Columbia Rockies are a totally uncontrolled environment. There is no one to pack the slopes or release dynamite charges. Control is limited to dislodgement attempts with skis by the guides. One must not only think about the slope they are skiing, but must also consider any other exposure which may bring a slide onto that slope. The biggest worry is an

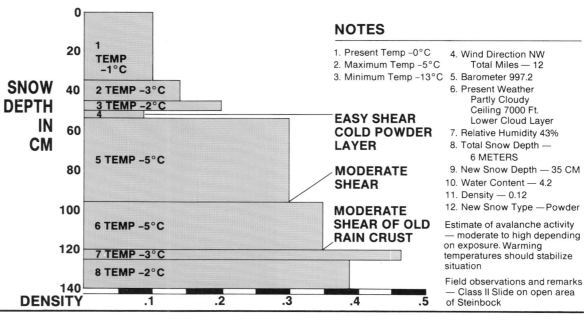

SNOW PIT DATA 3/15/84 STEINBOCK ELEVATION 6000 FT. ASPECT NORTH

SLOPE ANGLE 35°   SNOW TEMP. SURFACE –10.0°C

FORECAST

A series of frontal systems will move across the region in the next two days bringing warming temperatures. Precipitation will be intermittent and will increase ahead of the frontal systems.

SNOW DEPTH IN CM

0
1 TEMP –1°C
20
2 TEMP –3°C
40
3 TEMP –2°C
4
5 TEMP –5°C
60
80
6 TEMP –5°C
100
7 TEMP –3°C
120
8 TEMP –2°C
140

DENSITY   .1   .2   .3   .4   .5

EASY SHEAR COLD POWDER LAYER

MODERATE SHEAR

MODERATE SHEAR OF OLD RAIN CRUST

NOTES

1. Present Temp –0°C
2. Maximum Temp –5°C
3. Minimum Temp –13°C
4. Wind Direction NW Total Miles — 12
5. Barometer 997.2
6. Present Weather Partly Cloudy Ceiling 7000 Ft. Lower Cloud Layer
7. Relative Humidity 43%
8. Total Snow Depth — 6 METERS
9. New Snow Depth — 35 CM
10. Water Content — 4.2
11. Density — 0.12
12. New Snow Type —Powder

Estimate of avalanche activity — moderate to high depending on exposure. Warming temperatures should stabilize situation

Field observations and remarks — Class II Slide on open area of Steinbock unpredicted slide during a period of stability of the snow pack.

Studies go on all year. Avalanche prediction is in its early scientific beginnings. A five-step program is carried out two times a day every day by the guides.

1. Daily Weather Data. Snow and wind for the previous 24 hours are recorded along with the humidity data. Wind direction and velocity play a huge role in determining which slopes are loaded with snow and potentially dangerous. Temperatures and variations at altitude are also computed.

2. The forecast graph is a summary of what is going on in the mountains at a particular time. Sightings of avalanche activity from the previous day are recorded.

3. Snow Pack Profile. Daily snow pits are dug whenever possible. The different layers are recorded according to the density, type of snow, and the stability of each layer. The "Shovel Shear Test" is used to determine the ability of a layer to slide over the layers below it. Weak layers are usually caused by depth and surface hoar, sun or rain glaze, new snow or wind pack.

4. Field Observations. Each guide and helicopter pilot records sightings of avalanche activity in terms of location, fracture length and run out length. Cornice buildup and release is also recorded. This is entered on the forecast graph.

5. Slope Test. This method of ski cutting on representative starting zones or small rolls and slopes to get a final confirmation of the slope stability before skiing.

Snow pack consists of a number of distinct layers resting on a slope of a known angle. Strength and stress forces are computed from snow pack properties measured in the snow pit. Snow pit data includes density and temperature profiles, depth of significant layers from the surface, shear strength among

layer boundaries, and classification of the structure of the snow crystals.

Working with the famous snow physicist, Bill Harrison, Mike Wiegele has designed a system which has been relatively accurate in the mountains.

Constant refinements in techniques are always taking place. These men work year in and year out on these problems. Similar effective approaches are in use at CMH.

Calculations of which slope angle goes into tension during a given weather and wind condition involves a major part of Mike's and Bill's lives.

Before skiing is commenced on any trip, skiers receive basic training in avalanche rescue and survival techniques.

As in mountaineering, heli-skiing involves some danger. The rewards are more than I ever expected. I always listen carefully to the guides' instructions and never place myself or anyone else at risk to the best of my ability. As you can see from the pictures in this book, I have been able to enjoy some of skiing's finer moments. I expect to enjoy many more in the years to come.

Camera gear

In the best possible week of sunny weather a good professional photographer gets 5-10 images that are of publishable quality. In a sunny week 30-40 rolls of film are shot.

The average ski week has 1-3 days of sunshine and the photographer should be ready to take advantage of it. Never leave the camera in your room, thinking that you will take pictures at the end of the week. Weather changes quickly. Often my best shots have come on the first day of skiing; the rest of the week clouded in. Take advantage of the good light while it lasts. Also learn to work quickly–when the snow is good, the skiers don't want to stop.

This first section will be written for the amateur who wants to record his trip.

Cameras–Small full frame 35mm cameras are best. They can be tucked in a jacket to keep them warm and they don't require much fussing to get them to work.

MAIN RULES OF THUMB

1. Keep the camera warm. I've seen more film ruined because the camera workings or batteries froze. Carry extra batteries inside your jacket in case the ones in the camera start acting up. Also, if possible, keep the camera inside your jacket in an inside pocket or very well insulated outside pocket.

2. Bring lots of film. Compared to the cost of your trip, film is cheap. Shoot more than you usually do. Always plan to have at least four rolls of film with you. The best light is usually late in the day, and you don't want to be out of film.

3. Keep it simple–The more complicated the equipment the

more likely something will go wrong. The best camera is the Rollei 35. The automatic compact Minox or Olympus work ok also.

4. Film–Best film for prints–Kodak Kodacolor 100, for slides–Kodachrome 64.

5. Time to shoot–Morning and evening light brings out contrast and makes for dramatic pictures. However, do not fail to take a shot when you see it if it is something you want to record. The opportunity will probably not come again.

6. Action–For action shots use a shutter speed of 1/500th of a second or faster if possible.

7. Check out your camera in cold weather before your trip.

FOR THE MORE SERIOUS PHOTOGRAPHER

1. Camera–A 35mm single lens reflex with a motor drive is best. I've used Nikon equipment for years, but any major system is fine.

2. Lenses–For average shooting, a 35-105 zoom is perfect. It is compact and can be used in a wide variety of situations. To complete the outfit a 24mm lens and an 80-200 zoom are good. Use UV or skylight filters to protect the lenses and to keep excessive blue coloration out of the slides above 6000 feet. Special lenses or filters may be needed for certain situations.

3. Film–For most situations Kodachrome 64 is best. You may want to experiment with faster films for cloudy days. Use Kodak labs or the best possible labs to develop the film.

4. Batteries–Nicad batteries work great in the motor drives.

Recharge them daily with heavy use. Bring extra batteries for the camera meter. Keep the batteries warm while you are skiing.

5. Movies–The same principles apply. Keep the camera warm! It is probably even more important for movie cameras than it is for SLRs.

HINTS

1. Use new, fresh batteries. Test them yourself to be sure that they really are fresh.

2. Keep the camera warm if possible, especially if the temperature is lower than 20°F. You might wear it with a harness under your jacket. Cover the camera body with a lens opening cover and put the lenses in your fanny pack.

3. Check out your camera in cold weather before coming. If that is not possible, put the camera in the freezer at 0°F and then check it out. Run a roll of test film through the camera in this situation.

4. Bring an extra camera body in case of failure. Use a Rollei 35 as a back up.

5. Clean the lenses daily.

6. Daylight setting is f-8 at 500th of a second–midday in February or March. Remember this in case the meter malfunctions.

7. Bracket scenics whenever possible. Go 2 stops above and below. With cold film, color variation can be tremendous. Bracket action shots also if possible.

8. If you are shooting manual in bright sunlight, remember to open the lens 1-2 stops. Use a lens hood if possible to stop glare.

9. Shoot skiers with bright, colorful outfits. Dull colors make dull pictures.

10. Fanny packs (especially the Lowe pack) make the best storage system while skiing.

11. Polarizers don't work very well at high altitudes and cause you to shoot 2 stops slower.

12. Shoot action shots at 1/1000th of a second or faster.

13. Protect film in airport x-ray devices. Hand carry it!

14. Remember–your friends will do wild things for a good picture of themselves. Be creative!

Beautiful images abound
in the mountains; there
just isn't enough time
to record all of them

Photographs make trips come alive years later

IT'S NOT AS STEEP AS IT LOOKS – SCOTT ROWED – MOST MAGNIFICENT – CARIBOOS

"PEEK-A-BOO"

Mountains, snow, sun, and sky provide infinite variety

We hope that this book kindles
your spirit to explore these
mountain ranges next winter

THE END OF A PERFECT TRIP—"MILLER TIME" IN THE MONASHEES.

About the authors

Neal and Linda Rogers now live on a ranch at Butte, Montana. Both graduated from Albany Medical College as physicians. Linda is a pediatrician and Neal practices otolaryngology and head and neck surgery. Both have skied extensively in the U.S. and Canada. The photographic images were taken by Neal over the past eight years. A joint effort in writing, editing and planning this book has resulted in this first of a series of publications by the authors.

A HeliSki Poster And Selected Art Quality Photographs Are Available.

Send for price list to:

Earth and Great Weather Publishing
202 S. Montana St.,
Butte, MT 59701

If you're interested in an outstanding heli-copter skiing trip

we have had personal experience with . . .

Mike Wiegele
Cariboo Helicopter Skiing
Box 1824
Banff, Alberta, Canada T0L0C0
800-661-9170

CMH Heliskiing
Box 1660
Banff, Alberta, Canada T0L0C0
403-762-4531

Kootenay Helicopter Skiing
Box 717
Nakusp, B.C., Canada
604-265-3121

Marianne S. Lowrey
12032 East End Rd.
North Palm Beach, Fl.
33408

María & Alberto Battista
Catamarca 3445 - Olivos (1636)
Buenos Aires
ARGENTINA
54-1-790-3217

Neil Bregman
c/o Sound Venture Productions
219-126 York St.
Ottawa K1N 5T5
613-233-9320

Peter Dooher
135-3445 Uplands Dr.
Ottawa, Ontario
613-737-7229